31

CHRISTMAS *dates* FOR COUPLES

this

BOOK

BELONGS TO:

_____

 &

_____

INTRODUCTION

Christmas is almost upon us. The most magical time of the year! The streets are brighter, people are happier, and our hearts are filled with joy and warmth. Everything becomes more glorious and enchanting, as if pieces of magic are sprinkled all around. And we can't help but feel all Christmassy inside.

The Christmas season is a time of connection and is the perfect opportunity for you and your partner to come closer together and strengthen your bond. There is nothing better than celebrating and sharing your merriest moments with the one you love the most.

This book presents 31 Christmas date ideas for you to spread across the days before or even after Christmas. No matter how festive or cheerful you may already feel, these dates will add a ton of excitement to your holiday season and will help you make some great memories together.

Whether you're looking to add some romance to this season or have some extra fun, grow closer together or feel like kids again, lose yourselves in Christmas conversations or enjoy some playful competition, these dates have got you covered. Pick as many as you possibly can and make the most of this Christmas season.

How to Use This Book

This book contains 31 Christmas dates, making it ideal for having one date each day of this holiday season. They would work equally well on any chosen day, as long as you are in a festive mood or seek to get into the Christmas spirit.

The dates are in no particular order. You can skip around and pick the ones you prefer each time. However, to make better use of the dates consider choosing:
a.   "The Advent Calendar Date" (page 26) by December 1.
b.   "The Time Capsule Date" (page 70) and "The Reflection Date" (page 71) after the end of the Christmas season.

In the table of contents, you will find the estimated duration of each date. Consider this factor before starting your date to make sure you have enough time available and that you are up for it.

For the purposes of this book, one of you will be referred to as partner A and the other one as partner B. At the end of the book, there are dedicated pages for each of you. Keep referring to them when prompted.

Let's get right into it. And remember, it's the most magical time of the year. Start each date with an open heart and a positive mindset and something beautiful may await you along the way!

TABLE OF CONTENTS

TABLE OF CONTENTS

THE PLAYLIST DATE

Nothing can set the holiday mood like a good Christmas melody. No matter the occasion, a Christmas song playing in the background is always a good addition and can instantly get you into the holiday spirit.

Start the date by putting together your very merry Christmas playlist including ten of your favorite songs from old classics to the latest hits. Make sure to write them down on the following list before you move on to the next step.

PLAYLIST

1. _____

2. _____

3. _____

4. _____

5. _____

6. _____

7. _____

8. _____

9. _____

10. _____

Now that your playlist is ready, it's time to have some fun with it. For each song on your list, find a corresponding activity below. Spend the rest of the day doing them all and creating lovely new memories together while listening to your favorite holiday music.

S͟O͟N͟G͟	A͟CTIVITY
1.	Partner A sings this song to partner B.
2.	Partner B sings this song to partner A.
3.	You sing the song together.
4.	Kiss each other for as long as the song is playing.
5.	Dance together to the song.
6.	Partner A narrates their favorite story associated with this song.
7.	Partner B narrates their favorite story associated with this song.
8.	Give this song a different title.
9.	Vote for the most touching lyrics of this song.
10.	Recreate a scene described in the song.

THE SCAVENGER HUNT DATE

Who doesn't long to get in touch with their inner child and feel the excitement they used to experience in their early years? Christmas magic makes everything possible, so it's time to take advantage of it and feel like kids again.

Dress warm and head outdoors for a jolly and playful adventure. Go on a Christmas scavenger hunt around the town and race against the timer as a team. You have 90 minutes to find everything on your list. Will you make it?

Alternatively, go on a group scavenger hunt with some friends and see who reaches the finish line first. In this case, take photos of the items you locate to prove your victory.

SCAVENGER HUNT LIST

1. Decorative Christmas drums

2. Nutcracker

3. Silver bells

4. Christmas stickers on a window

5. Christmas snow globe

6. White mistletoe

7. Someone wearing red boots

8. Snowman

9. White gnome

10. North Pole sign

11. Gingerbread house

12. Tinsel

13. Candle string lights

14. Christmas lantern

15. Pink ornament

16. Advent calendar

17. Pine cones

18. Christmas candlestick

19. Toy reindeer

20. Wreath with red bow

THE CHRISTMAS LIBS DATE

Are you in the mood for being goofy and having a cozy Christmas date night from the comfort of your couch? Then this one is for you! Grab a pen and ask your partner for words to fill in the blanks with. Then, read the funny little stories you created aloud and share some laughs with each other. Take turns to fill in each story.

DECORATING THE TREE

After much _____, the _____ tree was selected and _____
          NOUN   ADJECTIVE   VERB

into the living room. Turning up the _____ to listen to in the
          NOUN

background, we carried down a _____ box of _____ to hang
          ADJECTIVE   NOUN

on the tree. As we both _____ into the box, we picked up the
          VERB

same _____ _____ to go at the very top. As our hands
   ADJECTIVE   NOUN

touched, our _____ melted. Our cheeks grew _____ and we
       BODY PART PLURAL   ADJECTIVE

began to _____. We looked up and _____ one another, feeling
      VERB   VERB

the Christmas _____ kicking in. We leaned in and _____ on the
       NOUN   VERB

_____. Forgetting all about the _____, we started to string
NOUN   NOUN

the tree. Adding the final _____, the tree was completed. We sat
          NOUN

down on the _____ to _____ the view, sipping on _____. It
       NOUN   VERB   DRINK

was beginning to feel a lot like _____.
                        NOUN

Snowy Christmas Morning

The best time of the year. Christmas morning. As I lay in my

_____, my eyes _____ to a blanket of _____ _____
NOUN   VERB   ADJECTIVE   NOUN

outside. It's snowing! On Christmas!

I make my way downstairs and am surprised to see a _____
                         SIZE ADJECTIVE

wrapped present under the _____. I _____ in excitement and
             NOUN   VERB

surprise as I thought we weren't exchanging _____ this year. Like
                    NOUN PLURAL

a child, I _____ towards the gift with a big grin on my face. What
   VERB

could it be? I _____ it, looking for a clue. You nudge me to open
      VERB

the present, so I start _____ it. I'm amazed to see a picture of
          VERB

the two of us holding a _____ at _____; one of my favorite
         NOUN   PLACE

memories.

A perfect picture for a picturesque Christmas morning. I _____
                       ADVERB

wrap my arms around you as I give you a big _____. I look around
                 NOUN

and see that I have everything I could wish for this Christmas Day. I

_____ "thank you" in your _____.
VERB   BODY PART

STROLL AROUND TOWN

There was a slight _____ in the air as we went outside to take a
NOUN

stroll into the _____ night. The _____ was falling _____
ADJECTIVE   NOUN   ADVERB

from the _____.
NOUN

Bundled up in our _____ jackets, we took each other's _____
ADJECTIVE   BODY PART

and began to walk downtown. Admiring all the _____ lights on
ADJECTIVE

the _____, we _____ in excitement.
NOUN   VERB

Even though the night was _____, there were few _____ out.
ADJECTIVE   NOUN

As we walked along, we could see _____ from inside each
NOUN

_____ home. We really felt the Christmas spirit as we _____
ADJECTIVE   VERB

further along into the _____ town.
ADJECTIVE

Even that was lit with beautiful _____. It inspired us to _____
NOUN   VERB

our own _____. We walked towards home after having a _____
NOUN   ADJECTIVE

evening.

Christmas was definitely in the _____.
NOUN

CHRISTMAS DINNER

Everyone is eating around the _____, gathered to celebrate this

NOUN

_____ holiday. I'm a bit _____ as this is my first time meeting

ADJECTIVE ADJECTIVE

your _____ family. As I pass the _____, I spill some _____ on

ADJECTIVE NOUN LIQUID

your _____. They laugh at my clumsiness. Oh, what fun! I let out a

BODY PART

_____ _____ as I start to also find it funny.

ADJECTIVE NOUN

The food is absolutely _____ and it wouldn't be a Christmas dinner

ADJECTIVE

without your secret recipe for _____. I look over at you and feel

FOOD

so _____ we get to spend this time together. It's not about the

ADJECTIVE

other people or the _____ food, it's about being in each other's

ADJECTIVE

company during the most _____ time of the year.

ADJECTIVE

THE TALK DATE

Discuss the following questions with your partner to spark enjoyable conversations about the holiday season. They will help you better understand each other and will effortlessly get you into the festive mood by fostering the Christmas spirit.

1.

You can experience the perfect Christmas evening. Where is it? Who are you with? What do you do? What is the background music?

2.

Which of your senses do you appreciate the most during the holiday season, and why? ,

3.

What gets you most excited for Christmas?

4.

This holiday season you are trapped in a Christmas movie. Which one is it ideally?

5.

What is a pleasant feeling that you only get during the Christmas season?

6.

How would you describe Christmas in five words?

7.

Santa is bringing you your most desired gift this year. What is it?

8.

What would be your partner's full name if they were named after their Christmas mood or habits?

9.

Would you rather skip Christmas next year or never experience a white Christmas again?

10.

If you became Santa for this Christmas and had only three people on your nice list, who would they be and what gifts would you give them?

THE BINGO DATE

Watching cheesy Christmas movies has become a popular holiday tradition. The predictable plots, the familiar romance, and the guaranteed happy endings make the perfect recipe for a comforting and joyful watch.

Hot cocoa	Carrying shopping bags	Dancing	Magical Christmas sounds	Meeting a love interest
Fireplace scene	Wise words by a stranger	Gift exchange	Strolling through town	Coffee shop scene
Baking cookies	Main character wearing red	**FREE**	Sharing Christmas memories	Missed kiss
Carols	Decorating for Christmas	Cute pet scene	Snow on the ground	Christmas getaway
Ice-skating	Pre-Christmas break up	Santa sighting	Hearing "ho, ho, ho"	Mistletoe scene

No matter if you love them or love to hate them, you can have some good time with them. Pick one to watch together and turn it into a fun bingo game.

Each of you choose one of the following cards and grab some markers to check the items off as you go. Whoever first crosses out five in a row wins the game.

Dancing	Wise words by a stranger	Gift exchange	Main character wearing red	Hearing "ho, ho, ho"
Carols	Decorating for Christmas	Fireplace scene	Mistletoe scene	Hot cocoa
Ice-skating	Pre-Christmas break up	FREE	Magical Christmas sounds	Christmas getaway
Missed kiss	Carrying shopping bags	Santa sighting	Meeting a love interest	Coffee shop scene
Baking cookies	Sharing Christmas memories	Snow on the ground	Cute pet scene	Strolling through town

The Santa Date

This date will be all about Santa. Get ready to pay a tribute to the big man in red and share some ho, ho, hos along the way.

Below, you'll find the activities for this date, starting with the indoor and moving on to the outdoor ones. Read through them to make sure the sequence works for you or rearrange the activities for your convenience.

How likely are you to complete all of the activities by the end of the day? Let's find out!

Activity No. 1

Write a letter to Santa explaining why you deserve to be on his nice list. Present the three best reasons you can think of. Then, pass your letter to your partner and decide whose arguments are more convincing.

Activity No. 2

Santa is thinking of renewing his formal costume and asks you to design a new one. Let your creativity run free and put your finest idea onto a piece of paper. Then, swap designs with your partner and discuss which one would look better on Santa. Pick the winner or debate until you reach a decision.

Activity No. 3

Take this mini Santa quiz and make it into a competition. The one who loses will have to shout "ho, ho, ho" in public when prompted by their partner.

Partner A

1. Which of the following is not one of Santa's original reindeer?
   a. Cupid
   b. Domet
   c. Dancer
   d. Vixen

2. What century was Santa born in?
   a. 5th BC
   b. 3rd
   c. 11th
   d. 19th

3. Where do French children leave their treats for Santa?
   a. On their nightstand
   b. By the fireplace
   c. Under the tree
   d. In their shoes

4. Where is Santa buried?
   a. Italy
   b. Turkey
   c. The United States
   d. The Netherlands

5. What do children in Denmark leave out for Santa?
   a. Cookies
   b. Bread
   c. Rice pudding
   d. Candies

Partner B

1. Which of the following is not one of Santa's original reindeer?
   - a. Cupid
   - b. Domet
   - c. Dancer
   - d. Vixen

2. What century was Santa born in?
   - a. 5th BC
   - b. 3rd
   - c. 11th
   - d. 19th

3. Where do French children leave their treats for Santa?
   - a. On their nightstand
   - b. By the fireplace
   - c. Under the tree
   - d. In their shoes

4. Where is Santa buried?
   - a. Italy
   - b. Turkey
   - c. The United States
   - d. The Netherlands

5. What do children in Denmark leave out for Santa?
   - a. Cookies
   - b. Bread
   - c. Rice pudding
   - d. Candies

Find the answers on page 76.

Activity No. 4

Head to the mall or just any place in town that you are most likely to find a Christmas photo booth. Your mission is to get your picture taken with Santa and be the silliest you can; sit on his lap, blow him a kiss, or play with his beard.

THE ADVENT CALENDAR DATE

Whether you're feeling crafty or not, this DIY project is one you can both carry out. Create a sentimental Advent calendar for your partner and add some romance to their countdown to Christmas.

Build excitement for each day leading up to Christmas Day by creating 24 love notes for your loved one. Pick one of the following themes, or come up with your own, and start writing. Once ready, give them to each other.

SUGGESTED THEMES

My sweetest memories with you
Reasons why I love you
The kindest things I've seen you do
Reasons why I'm grateful for you

Turn to pages 81-104 to find and cut some paper cards to write your messages on. Once ready, you can stack them facedown on top of each other with number 1 being at the top. Put each pile on your nightstands and draw one each morning as soon as you wake up. Feel the warmth of your partner's words and set the mood for another delightful Christmas day!

Consider the following ideas to take it up a notch.
* Use a pouch for each day of your Advent calendar and place a Christmas treat inside along with your love note.
* If you're both into arts and crafts, integrate your skills into creating a more fanciful Advent calendar to present your love notes with.

THE GUESSING GAME DATE

Christmas is the perfect season to find yourself playing fun games and reliving your childhood. On this date, you will play a ten-round guessing game with each other.

In each round, you and your partner will be something different, but both related to the holiday season. Partner A starts the first round by asking partner B questions that will help them figure out what they are. The questions can be answered only with "Yes" or "No." If the answer to your question is "Yes," then you get to ask one more. If the answer is "No," it's your partner's turn to ask a question.

Continue playing that way until one of you guesses what the other one is. Alternate who asks the first question in each round. Partner A and partner B should turn to page 77 and 79 respectively to find the relevant info for each round. Make sure you don't peek at each other's pages. If needed, cut them out and keep them close.

Winner of the game is the one who wins the most rounds.

THE CHRISTMAS STORY DATE

It's the beauty and magic of this season that give birth to the stories that fill our hearts with grace and warmth. Whether as a novel, a movie, or a tale, there is always something captivating in masterfully capturing the spirit of Christmas.

While there is no better time of year to pull out your favorite Christmas tale, nothing is more exciting and unique than creating your own. And that's what you are challenged to do on this date.

First, decide on your story's theme. Will it be about you two or something else? One of you will start by writing a sentence. Then, you'll pass it to your partner to write the next one. Repeat the process until you reach the end of your story.

NOTE: Stories are meant to be told, and so is yours! Practice your narrative skills and read your tale to your family or friends on Christmas Day. Wait for their reaction or ask for their feedback if you like. To have some extra fun with it, turn it into a guessing game of which run of events was whose idea.

TITLE:

_____

Once upon a time _____

_____

_____

_____

_____

_____

_____

_____

_____

_____

_____

_____

_____

_____

_____

_____

_____

_____

_____

_____

_____

_____

_____

_____

_____

THE END

The Watching Date

This date will take you outdoors on a stop-and-watch journey. Find a bustling place in town, sit on a bench, and watch life unfold before your eyes.

Focus on one thing at a time and absorb all the little details to make you more aware and appreciative of the present. Remember, it's the little things in life that matter the most. The all-pervading Christmas spirit will add a festive tone to your adventure and will fill your hearts with charm and joy.

As people go by, observe them closely and try to pick up on their stories. Share your guesses with each other and find out how similar your views and judgment are.

At the same time, keep an eye out to pick a winner for each of the following awards. Your decisions must be unanimous.

AWARDS

✳ The brightest Christmas smile

✳ The most stylish outfit

✳ The most impressive Christmas gloves

✳ The most adorable couple

✳ The most cheerful mood

THE LETTER DATE

This date will be a simple yet meaningful one, with minimum interaction but great sentimental value. Nothing fancy or complex; just the two of you writing a letter to each other to read on Christmas Day.

Sit opposite each other so you can share glances and smiles as you let your thoughts flow out onto the paper. Make the first part of the letter about this past year and write down all the things you are thankful for about your partner. Then focus on the future and finish your letter with your wishes for the coming year.

Writing gives our thoughts time to grow, making it easier for us to identify and lovingly express our feelings with the ones that matter the most. Letters from loved ones excite us all, filling us with anticipation to open and read. There's something magical about them that outweighs the words we speak. Create this precious keepsake for your partner and make your words stay with them forever.

THE NAUGHTY AND NICE DATE

On this date, you'll put yourself in Santa's shoes and you'll have to decide whether your partner has been naughty or nice. Fill out the following lists with some of the naughtiest and nicest things your partner has done over the course of the past year. Once ready, compare the two lists to determine if your partner deserves to receive a gift or be punished instead.

NAUGHTY LIST

NICE LIST

NAUGHTY LIST   NICE LIST

NOTES:

* Keep it playful and light!
* Find the gifts and punishments on page 76.
* Partner A fills in the first set of lists and partner B fills in the second one.

33

THE GIFT DATE

Get ready for a trip to your local shopping mall. It's time to do some Christmas shopping and put a smile on your partner's face. Your goal is to find the perfect gift under $10 for your partner and do it better than them.

Once you get to the mall, you get one hour to look through the shop windows and navigate the stores. Set a meeting point and start off your search independently. Take pictures of ten interesting and qualifying gift options as you spot them. Before the time is up, pick the best you could find and meet your partner at your meeting point. Keep your gift out of your partner's view if possible.

Head to a cozy coffee shop to enjoy your favorite drinks. Once settled, show your partner the pictures you took and ask them to prioritize the shown items in order of preference, starting with their favorite one. Once you are both done, comes the moment of truth! Who did a better job?

Winner of the challenge is the one whose gift has the highest ranking on their partner's list.

THE DRAWING DATE

Are you up for a Christmas-themed challenge that will show you how well you communicate with each other? If yes, then this one is for you!

Each partner will be given a list of ten Christmas-related items. Your goal is to make your partner guess what these items are by using your drawings. You can draw anything except for words and the secret items.

Take turns making a drawing for each item on your list. Feel free to choose the items in any order you like or pass if you get stuck. You have 20 minutes in total to complete the challenge. When time is up, count the items that you both guessed correctly, and you get your score!

Partner A should turn to page 78 and partner B to page 80 to find your secret items. Grab your drawing supplies and let the race against the timer begin!

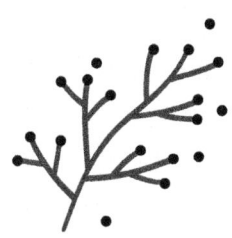

THE NEW TRADITION DATE

The holiday season is all about making memories with our loved ones. Christmas is packed with traditions that we cherish and long for each year. Putting up holiday decorations, gathering with family and friends, and savoring delicious Christmas food and treats are just a few that bring us together and help us celebrate with each other.

While there is something wonderful in celebrating Christmas in familiar ways, creating your own traditions will help you grow closer together and strengthen your bond. Establishing new holiday rituals that are unique to you and your partner, in addition to celebrating old ones, will breathe new life into your holiday season and make another reason to anticipate it.

Below, you'll find a few ideas to get you started. Pick one or more or come up with your own. Spend the rest of your date discussing with each other about your new Christmas traditions and the ways you could incorporate them into this holiday season.

NEW TRADITIONS

Create your own hot chocolate recipe and enjoy it on Christmas Day. Ideally, the recipe would be reflective of your relationship and a combination of your tastes.

Dedicate a day to delving into another culture's Christmas traditions. Pick your favorite one and make it part of your celebrations. Choose a different culture each year.

Put together a Christmas cookies platter consisting of your favorite recipes. Don't have any? Experiment in the kitchen and make a whole new date out of it. Give this platter a meaningful name and prepare it each holiday season.

Create a non-traditional dish to include on your annual Christmas menu.

Pick a random children's Christmas book and read it to each other on Christmas Eve.

Buy the most beautiful ornament you come across each year, regardless of whether it matches your decorations.

Create a personalized Christmas newsletter and mail it to family and friends. Include the highlights of the year and some of your favorite photos.

Write your own Christmas song and sing it together on Christmas Day.

THE WALK DATE

The smell of burning woods in the air, the feeling of cold air on your skin, and the flickering lights alongside the streets set a magical ambience perfect for the most romantic night walks this time of the year.

Taking advantage of this beautiful winter scenery, take a stroll around your neighborhood to watch the Christmas lights and decorations. Nothing feels more dreamlike than finding yourself in the middle of an enchanting Christmas setting and taking in all of its beauty and grace.

And while enjoying the sparkly surroundings would make a great date in itself, rating your neighbors' decorations and assigning relevant awards will add some fun and playfulness to your nighttime adventure. Let your first impressions narrow down your list of candidates but take a closer look at the details before you name the awards.

AWARDS

❋ The prettiest Christmas decorations

❋ The most expensive-looking Christmas decorations

❋ The most glamorous decorations

❋ The least impressive Christmas decorations

❋ The most tacky Christmas decorations

THE RANDOM DATE

This date will be one of those that you start without knowing what comes next. The only thing you need is to be ready for anything and commit to following the instructions. Are you up for the challenge? If so, follow the steps one at a time and let the fun begin.

STEP 1

Each of you should make a list of ten of your favorite things to do or experience on a typical Christmas evening. A few ideas to consider are smells, foods, sounds, visuals, and activities. Complete this step independently on the next few pages and make sure you don't peek at each other's list. Use a piece of paper to cover partner's A list when partner B fills in their own.

STEP 2

Each of you should randomly pick three numbers between 1 and 10. Read the corresponding items on your partner's list. Gather up all six items and make a list of them. Have you guessed it by now? The goal is to carry all of them out by the end of day. Will you make it? Start right away. There's never enough time when you're having fun!

<u>PARTNER A</u>

1. _____

2. _____

3. _____

4. _____

5. _____

6. _____

7. _____

8. _____

9. _____

10. _____

<u>Partner B</u>

1. _____

2. _____

3. _____

4. _____

5. _____

6. _____

7. _____

8. _____

9. _____

10. _____

THE MEMORIES DATE

Christmas conversations are always pleasant and heartwarming, especially when you're having them with your loved ones. Good questions can evoke cheerful feelings and bring back treasured memories.

This date will be all about reminiscing and sharing with each other some of your greatest Christmas experiences. Spend some time discussing the following questions with your partner. You will not only learn more about each other, but you will also pin down some of the merriest moments of your life.

Grab your favorite drink, cuddle up, and get ready to take a trip down memory lane.

1.

What is the best Christmas dish you've ever tasted?

2.

What is the most beautiful Christmas view you've witnessed?

3.

What is your favorite childhood Christmas memory?

4.

What is the best Christmas gift you've ever received?

5.

What is the best Christmas you've ever had? What made it special?

6.

What did you like the most about Christmas when you were a kid?

7.

What did your family Christmas tree look like?

8.

What is the most magical Christmas moment you have experienced and why?

9.

What are your fondest memories of Santa Claus?

10.

What did a typical Christmas morning look like in your childhood?

THE BAKING DATE

It's the sweetest time of the year, and this date will be one of your most delicious ones. You and your partner will get festive in the kitchen by preparing some simple yet tasty gingerbread flavored sugar cookies.

You will not only feel the joy of baking together but will also make it into a competition right before the end to spice things up a little bit and have some extra Christmassy laughs. Now, grab a few simple ingredients, wear your aprons, and get ready to make each corner of your house smell like holiday happiness!

You can use either the recipe below or any cookie recipe you like. Your challenge is to hand-cut some cookies while blindfolded, as you compete to create the best-looking ones. Each of you will have to hand-cut three cookies in different shapes (a heart, a stocking, and a gingerbread man) taking turns one at a time. You get two minutes for each cookie, and you can use any tool available except for cookie cutters.

INGREDIENTS

For the cookies
- ¾ cup butter at room temperature (or plant butter if vegan)
- ¾ cup granulated sugar
- 1 egg (or 1 tbsp plant milk and 1 tbsp corn syrup if vegan)
- 1 tbsp vanilla extract
- ½ tsp salt
- 1 tsp baking powder
- 2 cups all-purpose flour
- Spice mix: ground cinnamon, ground nutmeg, ground cloves, ground cardamom, ground allspice, ground star anise, ground ginger

Adjust the spice mix to your liking by adding your own selection of spices to the desired quantity and proportion. Suggested spice mix quantity: 1-3 tsp.

For the icing
- 2 egg whites (or 2 tbsp plant milk and 2 tbsp light corn syrup if vegan)
- 3 cups icing sugar
- 1 tsp vanilla extract

INSTRUCTIONS

1. Beat the butter and sugar using a mixer until creamy and smooth.

2. Add in the egg (or the plant milk and corn syrup if vegan).

3. Add the vanilla extract and the spices and mix them together.

4. Add the flour, baking powder, and salt and mix on low speed until just combined.

5. Cut the dough into four parts and roll it into balls.

6. Roll out the dough on a floured surface until it's 1/6" thick.

7. Place it in the fridge for 30-60 minutes.

8. While waiting for the dough to chill, gather any tools that might help you hand-cut the cookies and practice your cutting skills.

9. Once chilled, remove the dough from the fridge and let it sit for five minutes.

10. Take one of your rolled out pieces of dough and cut it into six squares of the same size (3-4 in). Then, use them to cut your cookies by hand. Each one of you will use three of these square pieces and will shape them into a heart, a stocking, and a gingerbread man. You get two minutes time to hand-cut each cookie while blindfolded. That's a tough one, so try your best! Shape the rest of the cookies using cookie cutters.

11. Bake them at 350°F for 10 minutes or until slightly colored.

12. Let them cool down completely before decorating them with icing. For the icing, just mix all the ingredients together and add extra icing sugar to adjust the consistency if needed.

Now that your cookies are ready, it's time to enjoy some! But first, you need to vote for the prettiest heart, stocking, and gingerbread man shaped cookie. Winner of the challenge is the one with at least two best-looking cookies.

THE HIDE AND SEEK DATE

Did you partake in hide-and-seek games when you were kids? If so, then you already know how exciting it is to think up good hiding spots or try to locate your hidden targets. If not, then it's time to find out.

On this date, you and your partner will entertain yourselves at home by playing hide-and-seek with a twist. Each of you should take down five ornaments from your Christmas tree. You are playing two rounds. In the first round, partner A should hide their ornaments anywhere in the house, and partner B should play detective trying to locate them while blindfolded. Partner A should give a hint about each hiding spot and navigate for partner B to ensure safety if needed.

Once partner B finds out all of the ornaments, the second round starts with you two switching roles. Winner of the game is the one who completes their round faster. So, don't forget to set a timer before each round.

Hints may include the following ideas:
* Near my favorite piece of furniture
* At the busiest corner of our house
* Where I spend most of my day indoors
* Near the spot we kissed last time
* Where I keep my favorite book

THE GIVING DATE

The holidays are the season of giving and unselfish love. Blessing the lives of others lifts your spirits as well. So, what better way to feel and share the joy of Christmas than by giving back and making a difference in people's lives?

Keep your heart open this season and give the gift of compassion to those in need. Be inspired by the following ideas and pick one or more to carry out. Then, spend the rest of the day trying to make it happen and grow closer together.

WAYS TO GIVE BACK

✳ Offer a warm meal, a food basket, or a bakery gift card to someone in need.

✳ Provide toys or books to a less fortunate child.

✳ Spend time with someone who has no family.

✳ Offer blankets and clothes to a homeless person.

✳ Donate to a charity of your choice. With so many charities extending across all kinds of different sectors, it won't be difficult to find one to support. Pick the one you relate most with and make a donation.

✳ Shop for a family in need.

✳ Fill some love packages with necessities such as soap, shampoo, wet wipes, tissues, gloves, socks, and water and give them out to the underprivileged.

Adopt that mindset and perform random acts of kindness throughout this season or all year round. You will do right and will feel right as well. It's a win-win!

Reflection questions to discuss with each other

✳ How would you describe the experience of uniting your powers for a greater cause?

✳ How did it feel to be generous and giving?

✳ How could you incorporate giving into your everyday life?

✳ What is something you learned about yourself or the world during this date?

✳ What is an act of giving that you could commit to performing as a couple on a regular basis?

THE MOVIE DATE

It's Christmas season, and what better time for a Christmas movie night than now? This date will be anything but ordinary and will let you come closer and play together while enjoying some screen time.

Below, you'll find the instructions for watching three movies, allowing you to turn it into a movie marathon. Pick one or more depending on the time you have available. Grab your favorite snacks, curl up together, and get ready to have some fun. It's movie time!

Movie No. 1

Pick a promising Christmas movie released this holiday season.

CHALLENGE: Kiss each time someone says "Christmas" in the movie. You may end up hating the movie, but you'll definitely enjoy the time you'll spend together sharing some love.

Movie No. 2

Pick a Santa movie that neither of you has watched before.

CHALLENGE: Before you hit the play button, guess how many times you'll hear the word "Santa" in the movie. The one who gets closer to the actual number wins the reward.

REWARD: Enjoy a candlelight dinner prepared by your partner.

Movie No. 3

Pick a classic Christmas movie that neither of you has watched before.

CHALLENGE: Each of you should make a list of ten of the most common Christmas items you expect to see in the movie. The first who checks all items off wins the challenge and gets the reward.

REWARD: Your partner will prepare your favorite breakfast the next morning you'll spend together.

	PARTNER A	✓		PARTNER B	✓
1.		☐			☐
2.		☐			☐
3.		☐			☐
4.		☐			☐
5.		☐			☐
6.		☐			☐
7.		☐			☐
8.		☐			☐
9.		☐			☐
10.		☐			☐

NOTE: If picking the movies is grinding, speed up the process by making a relevant search on the internet for each movie. Open the first page of the results and pick the first movie on the list you'll find. Skip to the next movie if either of you has already watched it.

THE PHOTO SHOOT DATE

Have some free time with your partner? This date will be a fantastic way to spend it. Psych yourself up for a day full of Christmas and some magical clicks. You are about to make some happy memories together and capture them for eternity through your camera lens.

From the list of Christmas theme ideas for your photo shoot below, pick the ones you like the most. Feeling extra confident and energetic? Then why not try them all and create an entire photo album out of them?

THEME IDEAS

Wearing ugly sweaters

Kissing under the mistletoe

Wrapped in Christmas lights

Decorating the Christmas tree

Getting cozy under the blanket

Surrounded by wrapped-up gifts

Feeding each other Christmas treats

Dancing to your favorite Christmas song

Walking around the Christmas lights in town

Ice-skating

Set a specific mood for a cohesive outcome or keep it spontaneous for a more casual result.

Mood Ideas

Joyful

Nostalgic

Whimsical

Romantic

Cheerful

Dreamy

Gloomy

Calm

Mysterious

Hopeful

Note: Would you like to add another twist to your date? Choose secretly the mood you prefer for a photo shoot theme and share it with each other right before the shot. Trying to combine them (if not the same), conveying the right message, and making it work as a whole will definitely be one of the hardest but also most hilarious tasks to attempt. Go ahead and give it a try!

THE QUIZ DATE

Have a cute and cozy date night with this fun Christmassy quiz. Use these lighthearted questions to test your knowledge about your partner and shine more light on their personality. Complete your quizzes individually and then compare your answers.

PARTNER A

1. Which color scheme would your partner choose for Christmas decorations?
   a. Green and orange
   b. Black and white
   c. White and red
   d. Blue and green

2. What outdoor activity would your partner rather do with you on Christmas Eve?
   a. Go window shopping
   b. Cozy up at a local coffee shop
   c. Go ice-skating
   d. Visit a live nativity scene

3. Which act would your partner choose to perform for their community?
   a. Singing Christmas carols
   b. Dressing up like Santa
   c. Running a cookie fundraiser
   d. Reading the Christmas story to children

4. How would your partner rather spend a snowy Christmas day with you?
    a. Throwing snowballs
    b. Building a snowman
    c. Sledding
    d. Taking a walk in the snow

5. Your partner can only listen to one Christmas song over and over for the entire holiday season. What will they choose?
    a. An old classic
    b. A jazz melody
    c. Carols
    d. One of the latest hits

6. What Christmas chore would your partner avoid the most?
    a. Taking down the Christmas tree
    b. Gift shopping
    c. Cooking Christmas dinner
    d. Untangling Christmas lights

7. Which main element would your partner choose for the Christmas decorations?
    a. Elves
    b. Angels
    c. Deer
    d. Snowmen

8. Your partner can only spend this Christmas Eve with one of these people. Who do they choose?
   a. Their boss
   b. Their neighbor
   c. Their accountant
   d. Their dentist

9. What Christmas tradition would be the least difficult for your partner to give up?
   a. Treats
   b. Decorations
   c. Family gatherings
   d. Gifts

10. Your partner must spend this Christmas abroad. Which destination will they choose?
    a. Norway
    b. Barbados
    c. The United Arab Emirates
    d. Japan

Partner B

1. Which color scheme would your partner choose for Christmas decorations?
   a. Green and orange
   b. Black and white
   c. White and red
   d. Blue and green

2. What outdoor activity would your partner rather do with you on Christmas Eve?
   a. Go window shopping
   b. Cozy up at a local coffee shop
   c. Go ice-skating
   d. Visit a live nativity scene

3. Which act would your partner choose to perform for their community?
   a. Singing Christmas carols
   b. Dressing up like Santa
   c. Running a cookie fundraiser
   d. Reading the Christmas story to children

4. How would your partner rather spend a snowy Christmas Day with you?
   a. Throwing snowballs
   b. Building a snowman
   c. Sledding
   d. Taking a walk in the snow

5. Your partner can only listen to one Christmas song over and over for the entire holiday season. What will they choose?
   a. An old classic
   b. A jazz melody
   c. Carols
   d. One of the latest hits

6. What Christmas chore would your partner avoid the most?
   a. Taking down the Christmas tree
   b. Gift shopping
   c. Cooking Christmas dinner
   d. Untangling Christmas lights

7. Which main element would your partner choose for the Christmas decorations?
   a. Elves
   b. Angels
   c. Deer
   d. Snowmen

8. Your partner can only spend this Christmas Eve with one of these people. Who do they choose?
   a. Their boss
   b. Their neighbor
   c. Their accountant
   d. Their dentist

9. What Christmas tradition would be the least difficult for your partner to give up?
   a. Treats
   b. Decorations
   c. Family gatherings
   d. Gifts

10. Your partner must spend this Christmas abroad. Which destination will they choose?
    a. Norway
    b. Barbados
    c. The United Arab Emirates
    d. Japan

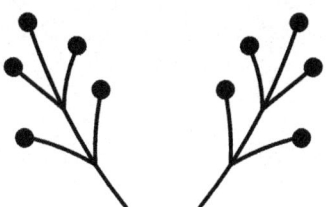

The Alternative-Christmas Date

What would Christmas look like without the jingles and the lights, the sleighs and the trees, the carols and Santa? It's hard to imagine such holidays, isn't it?

But let's pretend that all the festive elements that make up the Christmas spirit have been taken away. What would you replace them with to keep the joy of Christmas alive?

Think of the following questions independently. Once you've both given your answers, compare them and find out what Christmas would look like for each of you. Then, discuss which idea sounds better in each case and try a couple of them for this Christmas season.

Alternative Christmas

What would people decorate if not a tree?

What would people build in the snow if not a snowman?

What would people decorate their home with if not Christmas lights?

What colors would radiate the Christmas feeling if not red and green?

What would people wear if not ugly sweaters?

What would people decorate if not a gingerbread house?

What figure would share the gifts if not Santa?

What would people hang if not Christmas stockings?

What would carolers do if not caroling?

What would people cook for Christmas dinner if not the traditional dishes?

THE PAINTING DATE

On this date, get ready to have some fun with a little Christmas painting contest. No matter how artistic you are, this challenge is right up your alley! Being imaginative and thinking intelligently are the only skills needed.

This challenge consists of three rounds. Each round has a specific theme and each of you should create a painting based on that. Once you have completed all rounds, share your paintings with one or more mutual friends. Show them your paintings in pairs starting with those of round 1 and ask them to guess what they are about. Whose painting subject will be guessed correctly first? The one with two or more winning rounds also wins the challenge.

It's not the prettiest that wins in this challenge, but the one that better conveys the right message. So, grab your painting supplies and try your best to capture the essence of each theme.

ROUND 1	PARTNER A	PARTNER B
TYPE OF PAINTING	Abstract	Abstract
SUBJECT	Holy Night	Santa Claus
QUESTION TO ASK YOUR FRIENDS	What is this abstract painting about?	

Round 2	Partner A	Partner B
TYPE OF PAINTING	Classic	Classic
SUBJECT	The freezing air	The smell of burning wood
QUESTION TO ASK YOUR FRIENDS	What sense does this painting illustrate?	

Round 3	Partner A	Partner B
TYPE OF PAINTING	Classic	Classic
SUBJECT	Hope	Love
QUESTION TO ASK YOUR FRIENDS	What feeling is expressed in this painting?	

THE "TOP 3" DATE

Christmas is undoubtedly the most wonderful time of the year. But what makes Christmas magical for you? Go through these questions to dive deeper into each other's worlds and pin down a few things about yourself as well.

Fill in each box with three items. Partner A should write their answers inside the boxes on the left, and partner B should write their answers inside the boxes on the right.

❄

What are your favorite Christmas traditions?

❄

Which things would you ban during the Christmas season?

❄

What are your favorite Christmas activities?

❄
What are your dream Christmas destinations?

❄
Which Christmas-related things would you keep all year round?

❄
What are your favorite Christmas foods or treats?

❄
Which scents best reflect the Christmas spirit for you?

❄
What are your favorite Christmas movies?

THE AUDIOBOOK DATE

What could beat a nice movie when in search of a Christmas story to get you into the holiday spirit? Well, the answer is fairly easy — books, of course! Have you ever tried reading a book together? If so, then you've probably found out that it's not as easy or practical as you'd hoped.

But don't be discouraged. Audiobooks are a great option and probably an even better one. Pick a festive Christmas audiobook, get wrapped in each other's arms, and let your imagination create some holiday magic as you listen to the story.

Once you finish the book, return to this page to discuss the following questions.

1.

Would you give a different ending to the story?

2.

Who was your favorite character? Why?

3.

Which actor would you cast in the role of the main character if the book was made into a movie?

4.

What was the most Christmassy scene of the book?

5.

What title would you give the book if you were the author?

6.

What was your favorite part of the book and why?

7.

What are some similarities between you and the main character?

8.

Did any part of the book remind you of your own life? If so, which one?

9.

Would you recommend this audiobook to someone else?

10.

How likely are you to listen to more audiobooks together?

THE RIDDLE DATE

This date will take you on a search journey through the magic of Christmas. Solve the following riddles faster than your partner and win the prize.

Read together one riddle at a time. As soon as you make a guess, jot it down on the first line. Then, wait for your partner to make their guess and write it down on the second line.

Once you've both provided your guesses to all the riddles, turn to page 76 to find the answers. If you have both solved the riddle, the winner of the round is the one who solved it first.

PRIZE: Your partner should give you an extra Christmas gift before Christmas Day.

Riddle No. 1   ✳ I shine bright
                      ✳ I like to draw people's attention
                      ✳ I can show you the way

                      What am I? _____

_____

Riddle No. 2   ✳ I can be a great gift
                      ✳ I'm precious
                      ✳ I come in a single color

                      What am I? _____

_____

Riddle No. 3

* I live in winter
* I love geometry
* You can't hold me for too long

What am I? _____

_____

Riddle No. 4

* You'll find me in a flying sleigh
* I get opened and closed
* I look small, but don't be fooled by my size

What am I? _____

_____

Riddle No. 5

* Desire is my middle name
* I live in people's hearts and minds
* I need words to take form

What am I? _____

_____

THE TIME CAPSULE DATE

Once Christmas is over and the festivities have come to an end, you may be left feeling low and nostalgic. The holidays that just went past seem to have carried away all the joy and the excitement that was overflowing a few moments ago. But what if you could keep the spark alive and carry along the best part of this holiday season forever?

On this date, you will create a Christmas time capsule together to carry your greatest memories and capture your holiday feelings and mood. Use this keepsake for years to come to reflect on this Christmas and relive your best moments with each other.

Turn this into a Christmas tradition and add some extra anticipation to each holiday season. You'll both cherish it in the years ahead!

INSTRUCTIONS: All you need is a little gift box or any other type of box you like. First, fill in individually the memories list that you'll find on page 105. Then cut it, roll it, and optionally use some string to keep it in place. Next, grab an item that best reflects the spirit of this holiday season for each of you. Lastly, look through your Christmas pictures together and pick your favorite ones – one photograph each.

Once you gather everything, you've almost done. Place all your items inside the box and mark the year on the outside. Keep it somewhere safe and pick it up whenever you're in a wistful mood.

NOTE: A great alternative to the box is using a clear or semi-clear ornament as your capsule. In this case, choose some small sized items that could fit into the ornament and slip inside its top as well. Optionally, you could decorate your ornament using some ribbons and/or paint.

THE REFLECTION DATE

Christmas is the perfect time for reflecting on the year gone past. This process helps us gain insight about ourselves, take in the lessons we learned, and appreciate our blessings. Ultimately, we uncover and acknowledge the pieces that make up our life and shape our inner world and mentality.

So, before you jump into goal setting for the coming year, consider and discuss these thought-provoking questions to review the past and start the new year with a clean slate.

END OF YEAR REFLECTION

❄ What is your most precious memory from the past year?

❄ What is the most important thing you learned about yourself and about your partner?

✳ Which items did you check off your bucket list?

```
```

✳ What is the most important lesson you learned?

```
```

✳ What is a goal you didn't achieve that you wish to fulfill in the coming year?

```
```

✳ How has your relationship with your partner evolved during the past year?

```
```

✳ What has been your greatest regret in the past year?

✳ What made you feel excited and motivated this year?

✳ How have you grown as a person since last Christmas?

✳ What was your greatest accomplishment this year?

LOOKING BACK

You've now reached the end of this magical Christmas journey. Hopefully, this holiday season oozed with romance and joy, allowing you to create some beautiful memories together to cherish for years to come. Discuss the following questions to reflect on the dates you tried and highlight your most festive moments together.

* Which date did you have the most fun with?

* What was the most magical moment you shared with each other during these Christmas dates?

* What is something new you learned about how you can celebrate Christmas in different yet interesting ways?

* What was the most meaningful date you two had and why?

* What did you enjoy the most about trying these Christmas dates?

APPENDIX

The Santa Date

1 B 2 B 3 D 4 A 5 C

The Naughty and Nice Date

Partner A	Gift:	Punishment:
	Your partner will give you a one-hour full body massage.	You will give your partner a one-hour full body massage.
Partner B	Gift:	Punishment:
	Your partner will take you on a surprise date that will include three of your favorite activities.	You'll have to follow your partner to a place of their choice that you normally wouldn't choose.

The Riddle Date

1 Star of Bethlehem
2 Gold
3 Snowflake
4 Santa's toy bag
5 Wish

THE GUESSING GAME DATE

PARTNER A

1. Snow

2. Reindeer

3. Christmas stocking

4. Angel

5. Wrapping paper

6. Ornament

7. Advent calendar

8. Frankincense

9. Gingerbread house

10. Caroler

THE DRAWING DATE

PARTNER A

1. Sleigh

2. Snowman

3. Chimney

4. North Pole

5. Ugly sweater

6. Fireplace

7. Christmas lights

8. Bow

9. Jesus

10. December

THE GUESSING GAME DATE

PARTNER B

1. Nutcracker

2. Ribbon

3. Elf

4. Mistletoe

5. Eggnog

6. Candy cane

7. Christmas wreath

8. Myrrh

9. Bell

10. Tinsel

The Drawing Date

Partner B

1. Santa

2. Christmas tree

3. Wise Men

4. Church

5. Gift

6. Carols

7. Cookies

8. Christmas card

9. Candle

10. Turkey

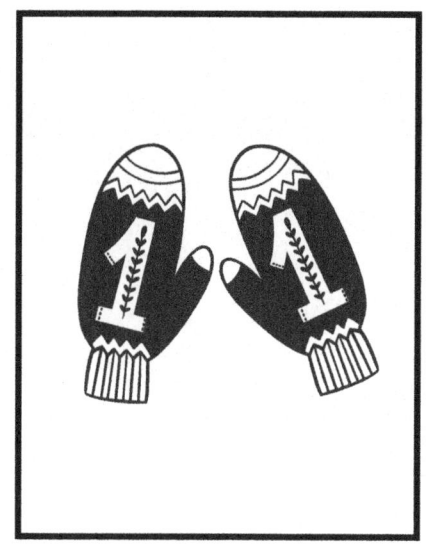

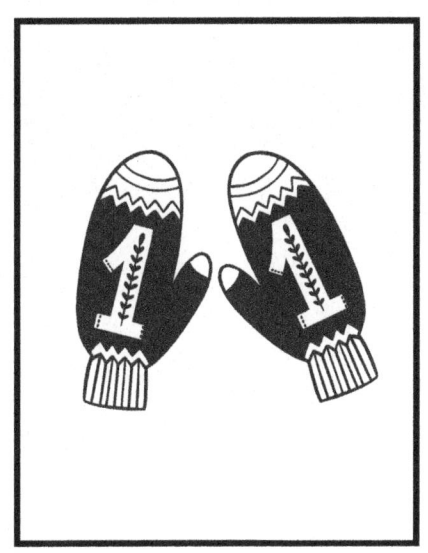

THE TIME CAPSULE DATE

MEMORIES LIST

My sweetest memory of us this Christmas
_____

This year in three words
_____

My Christmas mood this year
_____

The highlight of this holiday season
_____

My greatest wish for the new year
_____

MEMORIES LIST

My sweetest memory of us this Christmas
_____

This year in three words
_____

My Christmas mood this year
_____

The highlight of this holiday season
_____

My greatest wish for the new year
_____